USBORNE

All You Need To Know About

Going to School

Contents

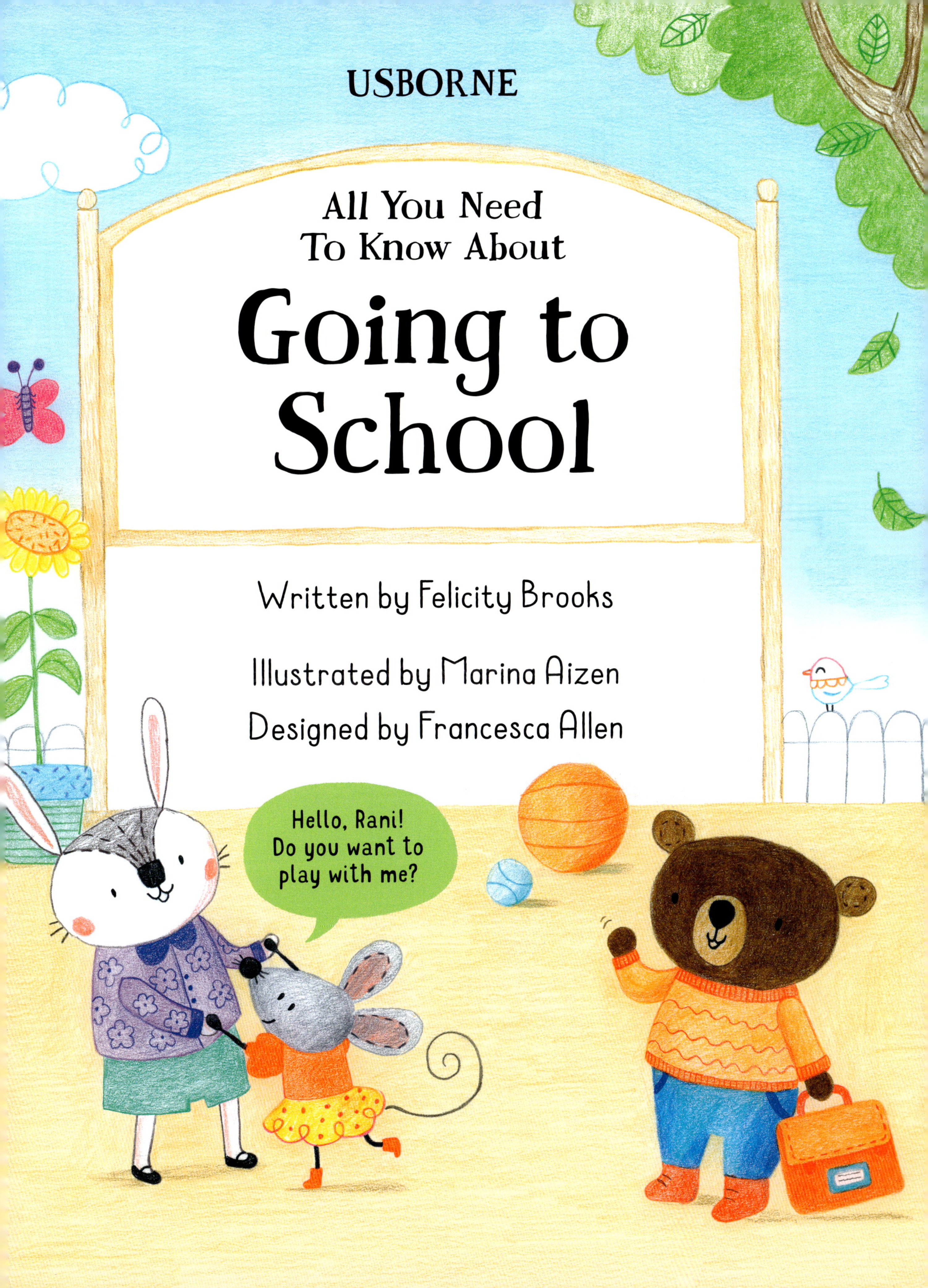

USBORNE
All You Need To Know About
Going to School
Written by Felicity Brooks
Illustrated by Marina Aizen
Designed by Francesca Allen
Hello, Rani! Do you want to play with me?

Getting ready for school

These are some of the things we wanted to know about before we went to school. We've put the answers to our questions, and lots more, in this book.

Before we go to school, we need to get dressed.
Do you know how to dress yourself?

sweater

vest

skirt

t-shirt

trousers

pants

shorts

cardigan

top

socks

shoes

Here are some things we may need to take to school.

Some of us
take our lunch
to school in
a lunchbox.

lunchbox

We need to make
sure our names are
on our backpacks.

backpack

Some schools
have special
book bags.

book bag

drink

bag

If we need special clothes for
PE, we take them in another
bag. (PE is games and sports.)

Our day at school

In the morning, we hang up our coats and go to our classroom for the register. Miss Honeybear, our teacher, calls out our names.

Miss Honeybear is very nice. She lets us do lots of fun things at school. We do painting, drawing, counting and playing with our friends.

At playtime, we go outside and play in the playground. If we
need the toilet, there are little toilets at school for us to use.

After we go to the toilet, we need to remember to flush
the toilet and then wash our hands and dry them.

In the afternoon, we often have storytime with Miss Honeybear.
Sometimes we can choose a book to take home to read.

Learning the names of colours

Which bottle of paint did I use for each picture?

I sometimes mix colours together
to make new colours.

Which paints
did I mix for
each picture?

green

purple

pink

orange

grey

brown

If I want to make
a colour lighter,
I add some white.

Which shape is which?

We can use shapes to make puzzles.
In the puzzle below, which is the odd
one out in each row?

In this puzzle, the last two shapes in each of these rows are missing.
What do you need to add to finish the patterns?

Time to count

When we can count to 10, we try learning all the numbers up to 20.
How old are you? Can you find the number on this page?

1 one

2 two

3 three

4 four

5 five

6 six

7 seven

8 eight

9 nine

10 ten

11 eleven

12 twelve

13 thirteen

14 fourteen

15 fifteen

16 sixteen

17 seventeen

18 eighteen

19 nineteen

20 twenty

Words for opposites

big

little

dirty

clean

last

first

top

bottom

outside

inside

sad

happy

Puff!
slow
fast
dry
wet
I'm short!
I'm taller than you.
short
tall
PARP!
Shhh!
quiet
noisy
Brrrr!
Weeee!
up
hot
cold
down

Lunchtime at school

At school, we can have a school lunch,
or we can bring our lunch from home.

Dressing up

After lunch, Miss Honeybear sometimes lets us play dressing-up. Can you guess who we are today?

Farm animal names

Neigh, neigh!
Quack, quack!
horse
foal
duck
ducklings
Eee-or!
goose
Honk!
Honk!
foal
donkey
Honk!
Oink, oink!
goslings
pig
piglets

The seasons and weather

We're learning about the four seasons of the year. Do you know what they are? Can you see what changes from season to season?

spring

summer

autumn

winter

We also learn the words for some different kinds of weather. Do you know all these?

sunny

rainy

windy

snowy

These are the names of some other outdoor things.

cloud **fog** **rainbow** **lightning** **mud**

Who's in your family?

Pets at home

We like talking about our pets.
Do you know the names of these?

Our bodies and our senses

We use our senses to find out about the world around us.

hearing   **smell**   **touch**   **taste**   **sight**

Nature names

We have been collecting things for the nature table in our classroom. Do you know their names?

It's home time!

At the end of a day at school, we take all
our things home with us. We know which
are ours by looking for our names.

Numbers to 10

Start at the big dot and trace over each number with your finger. Practise counting from 1 to 10.

1 2 3 4

5 6 7

8 9 10

Big letters

These letters are called capital letters. We all have a capital letter at the start of our names. Can you find your letter?

A B C D

E F G H

I J K L M

N O P Q

R S T U V

W X Y Z

Little letters

These letters are called lowercase letters. At school, we learn all the big and little letters so that we can write our names and other words.

a b c d
e f g h
i j k l m
n o p q
r s t u v
w x y z

What are we learning?

We're talking about all the things we are learning. Which of these things can you do? And which things are you still practising?

You might not be able to do all of these things yet, but you soon will.

Notes for grown-ups

This book is designed as a reassuring introduction to school and the things that children do there. There's lots to spot and talk about on every page and these important activities help children expand their vocabulary and encourage conversations about school.

Children develop in different ways and at different rates, so always try to go at their pace and don't worry if some of the things in this book take a little longer to learn than others.

Visit Usborne Quicklinks to find a selection of early years resources and helpful advice and ideas for grown-ups.

Children should be supervised online. Please follow the internet safety guidelines at Usborne Quicklinks. Usborne Publishing is not responsible for the content of any website other than its own.

Edited by Jessica Greenwell

Additional design by Yasmin Faulkner